Working Dogs
Assistance Dogs

by Mari Schuh

Consulting Editor: Gail Saunders-Smith, PhD

Consultant: Eileen Bohn
Director of Programs
Helping Paws Inc.

CAPSTONE PRESS
a capstone imprint

Pebble Plus is published by Capstone Press,
151 Good Counsel Drive, P.O. Box 669, Mankato, Minnesota 56002.
www.capstonepub.com

032010
005740CGF10

Library of Congress Cataloging-in-Publication Data
Schuh, Mari C., 1975–
    Assistance dogs / by Mari Schuh.
        p. cm.—(Pebble plus. Working dogs)
    Includes bibliographical references and index.
    Summary: "Simple text and full-color photos illustrate the traits, training, and duties of assistance dogs"—Provided by publisher.
    ISBN 978-1-4296-4474-7 (library binding)
    1. Service dogs—Juvenile literature. 2. Working dogs—Juvenile literature. I. Title. II. Series.
    HV1569.6.S38 2011
    362.4'048--dc22   2009051413

Editorial Credits
Erika Shores, editor; Bobbie Nuytten, designer; Marcie Spence, media researcher; Eric Manske, production specialist

Photo Credits
AP Images/Lexingtor Herald-Leader, Frank Anderson, 13
Ardea/Jean Michel Labat, 7
Capstone Studio/Karon Dubke, cover (collar), 11, 19
CORBIS/Markus Altmann, cover
Getty Images Inc./Erik S. Lesser, 15; Spencer Platt, 17
Newscom, 5, 21
Shutterstock/Steve Shoup, 1, 9

Note to Parents and Teachers

The Working Dogs series supports national social studies standards related to people, places, and culture. This book describes and illustrates assistance dogs. The images support early readers in understanding the text. The repetition of words and phrases helps early readers learn new words. This book also introduces early readers to subject-specific vocabulary words, which are defined in the Glossary section. Early readers may need assistance to read some words and to use the Table of Contents, Glossary, Read More, Internet Sites, and Index sections of the book.

Table of Contents

Helping People

Assistance dogs go
to work every day.
These dogs help people
with disabilities.

Types of Assistance Dogs

Guide dogs help people

who are blind.

These dogs lead their owners

across busy streets.

Hearing dogs help people
who are deaf.
They let their owners know
if the phone or doorbell rings.

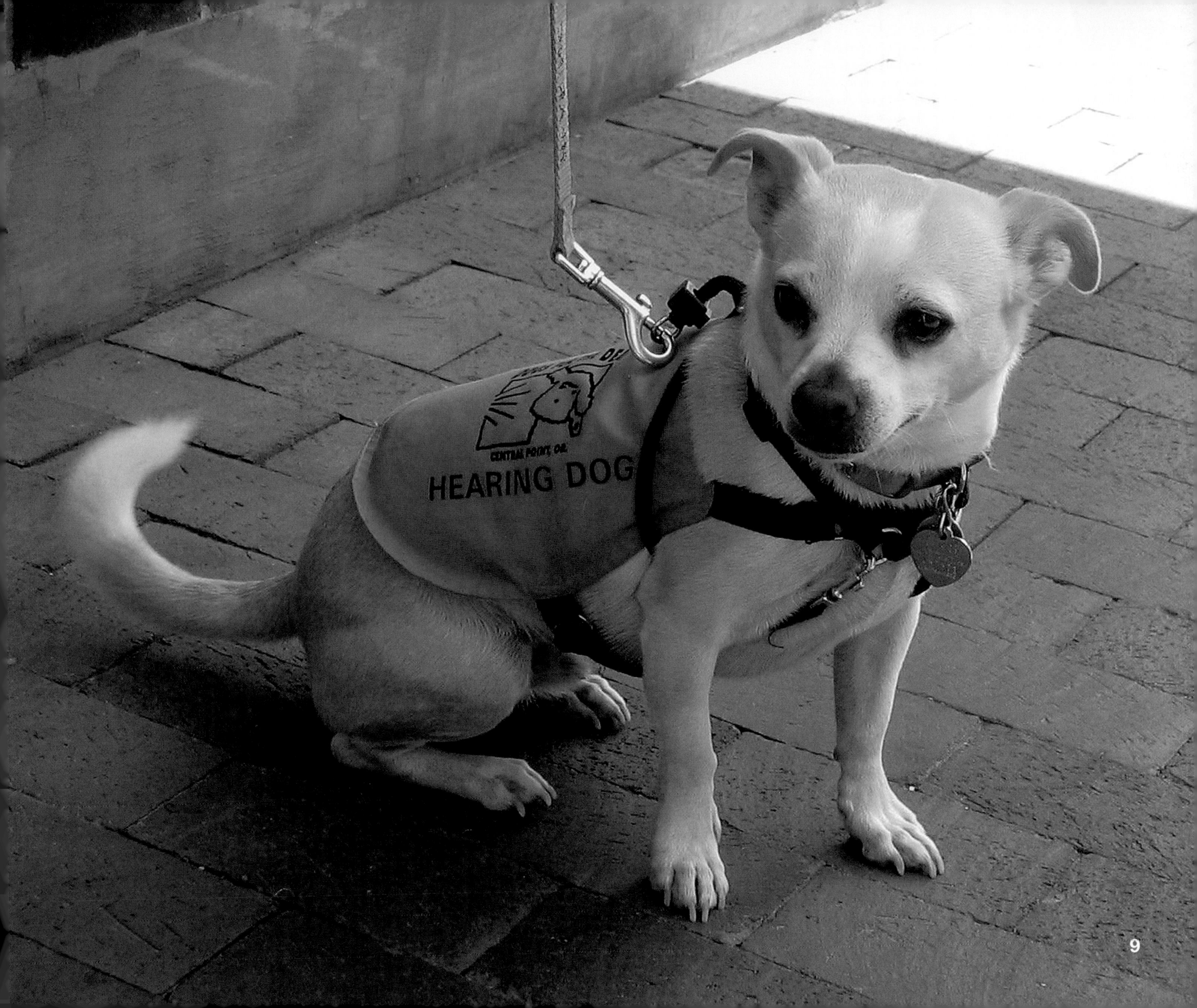
HEARING DOG

Service dogs help people
with other disabilities.
Some owners are in wheelchairs.
Service dogs pick up items,
open doors, and turn on lights.

Some service dogs help

people with epilepsy

or other medical conditions.

The dogs are trained

to get help for their owners.

Training

Assistance dogs train

for up to two and a half years.

They learn commands

for all their jobs.

Assistance dogs wear uniforms.

Vests, special collars,

or harnesses show people

the dogs are working.

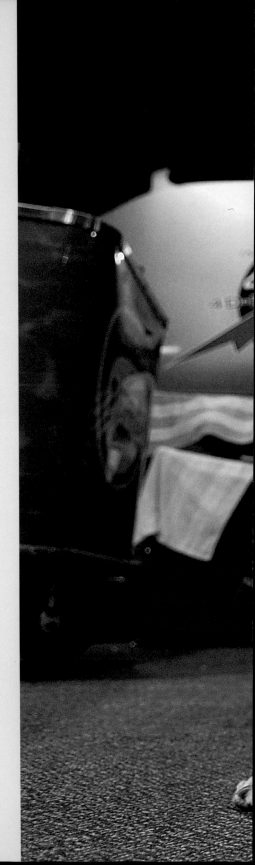

Assistance dogs need to focus on helping their owners. Always ask before petting or playing with a working dog.

Assistance dogs are strong,

smart, and friendly.

These special dogs help

their owners for many years.

Glossary

assistance—something that helps or makes something easier for someone

command—an order to follow a direction

disability—something that limits a person in what they can do; a person can have a disability because of an illness or injury, or they can be born with a disability

epilepsy—an illness that causes people to have blackouts or convulsions, called seizures

harness—a set of leather straps worn by a working dog when it leads or pulls

Read More

Barnes, Julia. *Dogs at Work.* Animals at Work. Milwaukee: Gareth Stevens, 2006.

Hall, Becky. *Morris and Buddy: The Story of the First Seeing Eye Dog.* Morton Grove, Ill.: Albert Whitman & Co., 2007.

Miller, Marie-Therese. *Helping Dogs.* Dog Tales, True Stories About Amazing Dogs. New York: Chelsea Clubhouse, 2007.

Internet Sites

FactHound offers a safe, fun way to find Internet sites related to this book. All of the sites on FactHound have been researched by our staff.

Here's all you do:

Visit *www.facthound.com*

FactHound will fetch the best sites for you!

Index

Word Count: 158
Grade: 1
Early-Intervention Level: 17